# COLLECTED WORKS

# COLLECTED WORKS

## CLERE PARSONS

Shoestring Press

All rights reserved. No part of this work covered by the copyright herein may be reproduced or used in any means – graphic, electronic, or mechanical, including copying, recording, taping, or information storage and retrieval systems – without written permission of the publisher.

Printed by imprintdigital
Upton Pyne, Exeter
www.digital.imprint.co.uk

Typesetting and cover design by narrator
www.narrator.me.uk
info@narrator.me.uk
033 022 300 39

Published by Shoestring Press
19 Devonshire Avenue, Beeston, Nottingham, NG9 1BS
(0115) 925 1827
www.shoestringpress.co.uk

First published 2017
© Copyright: Clere Parsons
© Cover image, On White II (1923), by Wassily Kandinsky

The moral right of the author has been asserted.

ISBN 978-1-910323-82-3

# CONTENTS

Preface – *'We Are Not yet Collected Works My Dear'*     1

POEMS (1932)     3
    Introduction     5
    Suburban Nature Piece     6
    The Winter Sunlight Splashes with Pale Gold     8
    Photogravure     9
    The Suave Blonde Is Paddling down the Skies     10
    Interruption     11
    Garden Goddess     12
    Restaurant     13
    'Never before Has Seemed Any Event…'     14
    Different     17
    'Living from Day to Day Provides No Clue'     18
    Who Stands Erect upon the Edge     19
    Staring at Shops with Vacant Eye     20
    When Trees Are Meaningless Empty Gestures     21
    Corybantic     22
    Some Melody of Words Continues on     23
    Sudden Death     24
    Last Poem     26

ADDITIONAL POEMS     27
    Paysages     29
    Débâcle     31
    Fragment from a Broken Ecstasy     32
    By Day the Green Wind Which Stirs     33
    Dancing     34
    English Winter Piece     35
    Plage Demimondaine     36
    Colour Photograph     37
    Suburban Naturepiece     38
    The Morning Smells Chaste     40

| | |
|---|---|
| PROSE | 41 |
|    A Plea for Better Criticism | 43 |
|    Editorial | 46 |
|    "These Gentlemen Call Such Writing Poetry" | 48 |
|    Purity | 51 |
|    Editorial Bouquet | 57 |
|    Obscenity | 59 |
| | |
| Notes on the Text | 61 |

# PREFACE – 'WE ARE NOT YET COLLECTED WORKS MY DEAR'

Clere Parsons (1908–31) belonged to that generation of writers known today as the 'Thirties Poets', who emerged together at the mid-point of the interwar years. Like many of them his background was decidedly upper middle class. Born in India to a Civil Servant father, Parsons was sent to a leading public school, St. Paul's, and then onto Christ Church College, Oxford where he studied alongside – although he seems not to have known – W. H. Auden. Contemporaries at Oxford at that time included C. Day-Lewis, Bernard Spencer, John Betjeman, and Stephen Spender. Reading Modern History, Parsons obtained a First and was awarded the Dixon Research Scholarship from his college. Aside from such prize-winning academic gifts, he was also to distinguish himself through his active involvement in the thriving Oxford undergraduate poetry scene. During his three student years – from which all of his written output stems – Parsons contributed to various small magazines, including the *Oxford Outlook*, the prestigious *Oxford Poetry* (which he edited) as well as his own short-lived effort *Sir Galahad*. Rather like Spender, at least in Geoffrey Grigson's vivid account, Parsons was, 'tall, slender, pale, fair-haired, with a feminine handsomeness... [and this was] allied to a certain mincing elegance.' However such a pallid and sickly complexion may have been a result of long-standing Type I diabetes and it was this which was ultimately to kill him. Having begun working as secretary to the Keeper of the Western MSS in the Bodleian Library, and whilst lodging in damp accommodation, Parsons soon caught a chill which turned to pneumonia and, with doctors seemingly unaware of his insulin-dependency, he slowly declined into a terminal coma.

Parsons was a keen admirer of contemporary American poets such as e e cummings and Louis Zukofsky as well as the recently discovered Hopkins, although his work is most deeply indebted to Auden, as "Who stands erect upon the edge" makes plain:

"Who stands erect upon the edge
Precipitate for new adventure
– Foregoes the sitting on the hedge
The timid facebothways composure" ("Who stands erect upon the edge")

There seems little doubt that had he lived Parsons' undoubted talent would have made him a poet of real importance.

This edition is the first to present the complete *oeuvre* of Parsons' writing, both his poems and prose. The majority of the poems are taken from his only collection – *Poems* (1932) – which was published posthumously at the insistence of Herbert Read. The others were printed in the undergraduate magazines mentioned above. Details of their original publication are included on the last page. Previously, Parsons' appearances in print have been limited to a 1989 selection by Cloudforms Press and those poems to be found in Keith Tuma's 2001 excellent anthology of British and Irish Poetry. It is to be hoped that the present edition will persuade new readers of Parsons' worth.

*John Howlett*

# Poems (1932)

# INTRODUCTION

I bespeak words
to please you and please
me (this pleasure shall be always ours, dear)
the accent I seek which
neither moth nor dust doth corrupt, but only taste I fear,
disciplines the pulse and rhythm of my speech.

Mallarmé for a favour
teach me to achieve
the rigid gesture won only with labour
and comparable to the ease
balance and strength with which the ballet-dancer
sustains her still mercurial pose in air.

# SUBURBAN NATURE PIECE

April who dost abet me with shy smiles
If I made bold by amorous fancy touch
Suddenly with my lips thy shining lips which
Are the smooth tulip and chaste crocus bulb
Lady be swift to pardon me this much

This day cannot long delay his choice between
Whether to be spring or remain winter still
– Behold the impetuous sun flings light like scarves
Of petalled lace to dazzle the ocean and
With silver lance our wintry moods to kill

Sweet month thou dost incite me to review
My fearful ship that hath all hopes in hold
O august barque of destiny bear me on
Safely those difficult and deep tides to where
No bird of fire shall steal my apples of gold

Throw open portholes and notice how the in-
Curved water at our wake is making a green
Drain smooth as glass but it must break
As the present breaks vanishing into the past
Pretending there the gayest days have been

Which is exactly not what either I
Or you really believe rather I swear
We begin here and now and shall throw no
Elegant flowers to sobbing yesterdays
We are not collected works my dear

Hail early nervous lucent appearing veil
Of tiniest veined leaf weaving a screen
To hide the bare and winter-weary black
Boles of the sentinel dejected trees
Wood ways shall soon be smelling earthy-clean

And here is the generous almond tree whose pink
Victorian skirt primly resists the wind
The ice-cream man who stands by the park gate
Is lifting towards the sun his commonplace
Simian face which is evil and grey-skinned

For with warm days also his trade revives
The children come with fixed and longing eyes
And with saved pennies as often as they can
To savour the small inverted cones of white
Ice cream surely consumed in Paradise

Amiable month unglove thy lovely hand
And with soft fingers conjure from the waste
Barren dry desolate sandstone of the mind
And stagnant pools of stale and weary thought
Rich water-lilies lightly to be embraced

By rainbow-tailed delirious dragonflies
Whose arrowing vivid sudden amazing flight
In summer stings the quiet bowls of shade
Bestirred by thee my thoughts again shall dive
Into remote space like violet rays of light

Listen my dears the skies are going out
Moonlight shall bathe the sleeping nenuphars
Musicians bring forth your violas-da-gamba
And stab my heart with bronze chords now that night
Gently is brushing the alarmed sky with stars.

# THE WINTER SUNLIGHT SPLASHES WITH PALE GOLD

The winter sunlight splashes with pale gold
The naked boughs which in the autumn shed
The pretty dress which is become rich mould
Maternal earth provides our daily bread.

The day reels to its feet like a drunk man
Stumbling over the edges of the world.

# PHOTOGRAVURE

    Io      Io      Io
      Sing the white birds
      Io      Io

Enter those tarnished woods
Where tensely
The summer broods.

Flystung in pools kneedeep to cool their hooves
Indolent and immobile the cows brood
Or lazily raise listlessly swish
And droop
        their tails

Climb gravely upon slow wings
Slower than Time utter your cries
La la you are holy birds
Dead sailors look through your eyes

    Pol-
    Perro    Io    Io
                    China clouds

Irresolute against heaven's Wedgewood blue.

# THE SUAVE BLONDE IS PADDLING DOWN THE SKIES

The suave blonde is paddling down the skies
O dream-stirred mind be steeled to meet the daybreak
Riding soft cloud she moves her shining thighs
Is unassuaged the limbs' imperial ache?

Is wisdom paralysed, reason afraid
Is the will asleep, shall shame avert her eyes?
Brittle are the quiet words the savants said
Preserve the imperilled body from surprise

Being is Destiny carried upon deep streams
Attempt change in vain, so Spengler says –
Ideals are but the stuff of empty dreams,
The words are forgotten with which the sage plays

The words are forgotten with which the sage plays
The suave blonde is paddling down the skies
But those alive in pagan antique days
Prayed to superb and curvilinear ladies.

# INTERRUPTION

The deep sun leisurely with mottled gray –
plumed wings closefurls the stippled day
in which they tentatively their souls paraded
in bodies attached by surest threads of silk
like monocles they dangled for effect;
each in ornate deliberate words bedecked
dancing attendance in slow modes of speech
in pauses rich to encourage confidence…
No hurry at all no hurry let the words fall
plumb, and roll gravely each like a cannon-ball
dislodged from proud pedestal or monument
gathering pace down dusky slopes of sense.
Time to gesture with hands, time to exhibit
how subtle and fine is thought it will not fit
(sometimes) into those labelled grooves of sound
we docket Latin, French, German, English…
Memory obfuscates and fancy obscures
also these sentences which slacken and pause;
causeless intrude the Quarter Boys of Rye
and early golfers walking on Camber dunes.

# GARDEN GODDESS

Cool is the wind which laps the leaves
And fans me to sleep. The drowsy hours
Curl round my head like heavyscented flowers
Whose rare perfume with every breath I breathe

The lake by lazy swans patrolled
Fluidifies her lovely line;
Fingers disturbed in that blue calm, divine
How cold in champfered folds the marble flows

Now joy's cartographer I trace
My acres of gay and wellbeing's land
O my summer be music be Proust and Sisley and
With me in the dead season, pastoral days.

# RESTAURANT

Into infinity the lights retreat
where parallel lines ought to but never meet…
The gentleman has fixed a date,
That's why he wears such a smile upon his face.
How he stares at nothing like a philosopher;
the waitress giggles and twists her hands together.
'I hope' sighing, 'the weather will keep fine.
But then we can always arrange another time.
The fun-fair's never much fun in the rain.'
'Certainly if it rains,' he smiles again,
'Certainly if it pours, we can stay indoors.'

Nature has her disadvantages of course.

# 'NEVER BEFORE HAS SEEMED ANY EVENT…'

I

Never before has seemed any
Event to bear so keen
An edge, to strike so clean the blow
Which from what was what is abruptly cleaves

This scene is frequent on the screen
Opening a letter then holding it between
Lax finger and thumb
It is like the snapping of a violin string
When the shock comes:
A sudden break in the running of the dream machine

By custom obedient the tongue utters 'Read this'
But the mind is dumb

Then the dizzy will
Struggles to be free, free
Of floor tilting walls reeling and ceiling
Or it may be none of these
But merely senses all,
Forms amorphous grey and inimical

'It is impossible, it cannot be'
In a new world he stands at bay
Facing a bayonet charge of words and reading
Reading
Hoping against hope they may
Deliver him still another meaning

## II

Then to begin to reckon chances, living
On hopes deferred, fitful and fugitive
With each move shadowed by the sly detective
Conditional If who governs every thing

Calamity is cold, refusing food
Each chance way out the imprisoned mind pursues
Turns cul-de-sac and aimless avenues
Bloodchilly echo 'This will be no good'

The ducal day bows long beneath his blue
Late darkening roof in two minds to be gone;
But now my thoughts forsake the summer and sun
To flowers and frocks become indifferent too

## III

Where, upon slumberous boughs they sit
  Preening their silver wings and sing
All summer in a day of song
– Small favoured Birds of Paradise
Is no place where you or I have been
Save in those shining secret ships
The galleons of our deepest dreams

But then set sail for coral reefs
And Islands where the dark palms guard
And mangroves fence the dusky beach –
There dawn brings but renewal of peace
And day's return is not this hard
  Hammer of anguish, this 'Repeat'
Drear labours of same thought, same speech

## IV

At the base of thought
At the core of being
This toxin runs to ruin
And poison the mind's calm

'Fortune's a fickle jade'
'Time heals all wounds…'
Conversing in platitudes
And waiting for what comes

Effort to move, to loose
Lethargic mind which values
Ritual of coffee and spoons
But anger is no use

To fall-to and abuse
The fools who rule by rule
Of thumb number and rote?
– But anger is no use

O arrive Time quickly when
This grief shall diminute
– A ship crossed and beyond
Hull-down, the lone sea's curve.

# DIFFERENT

Not to say what everyone else was saying
not to believe what everyone else believed
not to do what everyone else did,
then to refute what everyone else was saying
then to disprove what everyone believed
then to deprecate what everybody did,

was his way to come by understanding

how everyone else was saying the same as he was saying
believing what he believed
and did what doing

# 'LIVING FROM DAY TO DAY PROVIDES NO CLUE'

Living from day to day provides no clue
For certain happiness – it is a shallow
Youngster philosophy and easy to see through
Sirs, we know what usually it comes to –
The drunkard's bliss, the braggadocio

'Admire me now triumphant over virtue'
The rake's bravado and tedious libido
Gin in small hours, praise for the cunning ruse

Nor can you live by glimpses of the 'True'
And 'Beautiful', snapshotting scenery;
However slick, neither will the kodak do

See gaunt and curt to luminary sky
Rear the gas drums the guardians of the city
– But emblems of elder power have passed by

Survey the ruined bridge, the crumbled tower,
Now homes for owls the desiccated trees
Which threw deep shade for feudal ladies leafless
Conjured a past from books of history

Reveal the narrow lusts the mean the sour
Rancid intrigues, the base servility

And till the day of doom continue too
Heads in the sand ostriches in a row
Far easier so, to do as others do.

# WHO STANDS ERECT UPON THE EDGE

Who stands erect upon the edge
 Precipitate for new adventure
– Forgoes the sitting on the hedge
 The timid facebothways composure

 Is hero too with wizard sword
 His perilous dignity is sure
– The master of a green accord
 Between flesh and the pulse of nature.

# STARING AT SHOPS WITH VACANT EYE

Staring at shops with vacant eye
With painted lips to mesmer glances
The feminine show, the finery

By which of two being kept enhances
Chances of grander in the next corner
Weighs pros and cons, gauging the consequences

Whether to live or business instinct give
The ampler rein, the longer tether, whether
In brief not to leave climbing and live.

## WHEN TREES ARE MEANINGLESS EMPTY GESTURES

When trees are meaningless empty gestures
Of earth's hardness and dumbness, December numbness
And desolate mood and sullen occasion shares

When timid ejaculation of rose damns
The hurrying hostile skies which threaten snow
And threaten a deeper loneliness for some

Answer me devoted but idle servant of my will
Muse, that I sing how one that was lost but is found
Heart warmly cockled, enjoys such a winter nightfall

# CORYBANTIC

Closing our books we walked into the air
It was the touch of life the genuine sense
Of the old part played as a new adventure
Future and past merged in the present tense

Blow when you will according to your nature
Eager March wind promise of vernal scent
Pagan in youth not unnaturally her
Demonic limbs this close constraint resent

# SOME MELODY OF WORDS CONTINUES ON

Some melody of words continues on
Over and above the words in which I think
And which the outer being is based on

If once within the bounds of meaning it came
I might enclose within a verbal system
This opulent lovely tongue that has no name

No rules of grammar, no place for adverb
No active and passive, no paradigm
Not even the primal and primordial verb

It is the original rhythm whence speech sprung
The dog feels too before the fire which burns
These crazy flames his deft thought leaps among.

# SUDDEN DEATH

I

Strip me of outer selves, strip off each layer
Plunge in my flesh your silver-hilted knife
Hold me with your cold detecting eyes
Stretch me upon your table, lay me bare.

If we go home now at once, we shall have time
Before the guests arrive, before the clatter
Of cups and saucers, rattle of teaspoons,
    Aunt Martha saying 'Poor thing! She's passed her prime.'
(Aunt Martha cannot face the looking-glass)
And Uncle Jasper with his monocle
Telling wide-eyed Stella how he shot the tiger,
And had she seen anything, seen anything
of Puffinger?
'Yes, one morning in the Via Tornabuoni
He had been lately changed into a zebra
And had already counted up to nine
When the magician broke his wand, the enchantment failed.
So he remained a zebra, unpopular,
Unpopular and avoided by his fellows.
Until one day, Bol the astronomer
Travelling that way, trapped him into a cage
And made him dance the Charleston on two legs
And they played the Carolina Blues
And all the native women rolled their hips
And zebra danced, and Bol twirled round and round
And then the lights went out and Puffinger
Issued, a little pale, from out the cage.

If we go now at once, there will be time
Before dusk falls, to reach the narrow cave
Where you will find your coat, your own fur coat
To keep you warm, and three electric lamps
Which you must turn together on my face

And I shall tell you all
        Everything!        Everything!
If I should stumble a moment, on my lips stammer
There are three apples and a pot of cream
I have placed upon the shelf, which I must eat.
Then I will start again – only one chance.
If you can stand all that I have to say,
When you have heard how all my family
Have lived with ghosts these many centuries –
How dangerous your own life will be.
How you will have to face the dragon's brood
That hovers round me like a following curse.
If you can stand all that I have to say,
Then there is nothing to come between,
We shall be soul-bare, and you shall marry me.

II

She lies so still upon the giant bed
Paler than death, the pale ghostly sheen
Is round her now. No need to prop her head.
She is stiller now than she has ever been.
The nurse and I alone in the quiet room,
  Make no sign no movement. We too are half dead.
The snow falls in the gloom –
And the thin hands upon the bedspread
Will never clutch again against their doom.

# LAST POEM

She does not choose to tread that way of faith
Which once she trod in plain simplicity
And duty. Now shower down your pity

Or make her the victim of your wrath and warn her
'Arrogant fool you will return in time
Sorry for your vulgar self-sufficiency'

Pray for her then as one who dared incur
The anger of every god and each creator
But who revered the mind's integrity
Whose hand was against strife
Whose love for the lowly.

# Additional Poems

# PAYSAGES

I

Flowers are twisted by desire
madness has filled
                the jaundiced universe.

The pollards writhe
like an eastern dancer
                rippling her limbs.

But here the waves are stilled,
The muscles petrified.

Genius and lunacy obey their laws.

II

Now in your mind my image has become blurr'd,
I must forgo the pleasure to prolong
the hazardous enterprise whose being stirr'd
my broken particles of thought to song.

These leaves are thick with honey from the moon.
The branches drip their clotted cream…
There are still virgins in cool places,
there are still virgins to be found.

Ladies and gentlemen, observe
my midsummer mind float like a fire-balloon!

## III

The Tuscan landscape is severe
and chaste, after our loose littered scene.
Here are no Rufus oaks to mar
the even march and regular
ascent into the Apennines
of amicable vines.

Tall cypresses that stab the sky,
like old men talking after church,
sadly and solitary stand.

## IV

I cannot bear the thought of winter now.
The shortening days precipitate my mind
to restlessness and gloom…

Did you remark
Brueghel will render luminous the darkest day?

We are too much a nexus of live wires.
Come, gather round
the seasonable fires.

## DÉBÂCLE

Out of the lion's mouth the present comes.
Zarathustra! Here is your hour.

Into the nursery at noon
came Zarathustra and the supermen.

Fabulous giants, what is it you have found?

A child asleep upon the windowsill
and on the untidy floor,
*grinning lions stuffed with straw,*
*wooden doves.*

# FRAGMENT FROM A BROKEN ECSTASY

Run, potbellied,
swing your gold chain, your seals –
run with your overcoat open,
pale homunculus.

– The day's accountancy is done,
    Now borne above the world we ride
towards the debile winter sun
    where heaven's argosies collide.

Beneath me in the windy stir
    newspaper-sellers advertise
the death of a philosopher
    by unintelligible cries.

Lost in what corner of the maze,
    with mine already dyed subfusc,
who is it weeps the vanished days,
    the tawny hair in honey'd dusk?

# BY DAY THE GREEN WIND WHICH STIRS

by day the green wind which stirs,
lady, the tranquil summer, brings
elusion from the breath of wallflowers
and from the pain of fierce geraniums;

but you being firm upon the scented earth,
the wind is but a cloak to wrap you in;
the invisible waves follow but your curves
and while I trace the pattern of sea-gulls

somehow the grace of these accustomed birds
and their suave admirable contempt of time
answer the steady pulse within your heart;
then the alert beauty of your eyes

throws such a flame even in this white day
as will light my tatter'd clumsy mind
towards your soul shining like a sword
close-kept behind the innermost veil of things.

# DANCING

opening and casting a
shutting glance CHARLESTON her
knees, wobbling CHARLESTON her
head I hope she bites CHARLESTON her
tongue. She

(whose girlfriend? why that one throwing
with such a studied gesture of boredatease
ringS of blue smokE bedad he's an Aristo
'Wherever the Best
People meet, you
know')

seems strangely to prefer the jew Gayboys

now let's think what we shall throw
what
   do
      you
         think, a
bomb? No let me suggest a Commode

                among all these

sleek marionettes whose waste would keep God knows
many a man on more than bread and cheese
and many a better fellow who's out-at-elbows.

# ENGLISH WINTER PIECE

the stark country which flies against us is
indigo darkness and sharp cold
the mauve banks and the dull jade
are now night's starred and inky veil

these boughs which loom within our rays
are bare brown bleaker than old maids
they stretch gawkily above the cross-roads
stiffer than Long John Silver's leg

into pools of dim dark into the vast phleg-
matic
silence

      (by us at what peril disturbed)

'RIDE-A-COCK-HORSE' I said –

but I saw beyond the lonely house
ride-like-the-wind a ghostlier horse instead.

# PLAGE DEMIMONDAINE

    this
      young
         Adonis
           who with such yellow hair admires
the suavelypaced Levantine mannequin
'En vacances, aussi, oui, monsieur, au bord de la mer'
'Shall we (He says) since the sun is so hot undress and bathe
over there beyond the dark rocks where
the green facets crinkle into foam,'

        hoping to appropriate his fifth this August
VENUS ANADYOMEN –
e which means
risingfromthesea (the others all
were giggling blond bathingbelles)

because this place is full of moneyed young men
and indolent phallophil idleminded girls.

# COLOUR PHOTOGRAPH

io    io    io
  Sing the white birds
io    io    io

implacably the sun burns

enter these tarnished woods
where scarcely
the Summer moves

flystung in pools kneedeep to cool their hooves
indolent and immobile the cows brood
or
lazily raise
listlessly swish    and droop
their tails

(climb gravely upon slow wings
slower than Time    utter your cries
La, la you are holy birds
dead sailors look through your eyes)

Pol-
Perro    io    io

                      china clouds
irresolute against heaven's Wedgewood blue

# SUBURBAN NATUREPIECE

April who dost abet me with shy smiles
if I made bold by amorous fancy touch
suddenly with my lips thy shining lips which
are the smooth tulip and chaste crocus bulb
lady be swift to pardon me this much

this day cannot long delay her choice between
whether to be spring or remain winter still –
behold the impetuous sun flings light like scarves
of petalled lace to dazzle the ocean and
with silver lance our sombre moods to kill

sweet month thou dost incite me to review
my fearful boat that has all hopes in hold
O august barque of destiny bear me on
safely those difficult and deep tides to where
no bird of fire shall steal my apples of gold

throw open portholes and notice how the in-
curved water at our wake is making a green
drain smooth like glass but it must break
as the present breaks vanishing into the past
pretending there the gayest days have been

(which is exactly not what either I
really believe no more do you I swear
we begin here and now and shall throw no
elegant flowers to sobbing yesterdays –
we are not collected works my dear)

hail early nervous lucent appearing veil
of tiniest veined leaf weaving a screen
to hide the bare and winterweary black
boles of the sentinel dejected trees
woodways shall soon be smelling earthy clean

and here is the generous almond tree whose pink
Victorian skirt primly resists the wind –
the ice-cream man who stands by the parkgate
is lifting towards the sun his commonplace
simian face which is evil and greyskinned

for with warm days also his trade revives
the children come with fixed and longing eyes
and with saved pennies as often as they can
to savour the small inverted cones of white
icecream surely consumed in Paradise

amiable month unglove thy lovely hand
and with soft fingers conjure from the waste
barren dry desolate sandstone of the mind
and stagnant pools of stale and cloudy thought
rich waterlilies lightly to be embraced

by rainbowtailed delirious dragonflies
whose arrowing vivid sudden amazing flight
in summer stings the quiet bowls of shade –
bestirred by thee my thoughts again shall dive
into remote space like violet rays of light

listen my dears the skies are going out
moonlight shall bathe the sleeping nenuphars –
musicians bring forth your violas-da-gamba
and stab my heart with bronze chords now that night
gently is brushing the alarmed sky with stars.

# THE MORNING SMELLS CHASTE

the morning smells chaste I
chance ab-
ruptly into morning which smells the middle ages
(Gothic cathedrals the tombs of crusaders and
the wounding
               ache
of cold
stone) against these twists
of flimsy and pink cloud the tall
spire of St. Mary's Church

dominates chimneys which utter thin smoke
and jumbled roofs.

# Prose

# A PLEA FOR BETTER CRITICISM

Here, Critic, is the harvest of OXFORD POETRY for 1928. We have gathered and bound it; 'tis for you to appraise it. Will you but cast a glance of your expert eye over our tender crop and dismiss it from your attention with some routine formula of congratulation or contempt? Or can you we hope that you will sift and judge the grain, if grain there be? We do not shrink from a threshing, nor resent the winnowing blast of criticism however searching it may prove. Rather we would provoke it, believing that for a young poet sound criticism is the best, if not the only, reward (*pace* our publisher) he can look to win. But can we hope? At least we can provoke.

Nothing in the world of letters is more noticeable at the present time than the paucity of good poetry, unless it be the paucity of good criticism.

The Georgian movement, which was in reality the swan-song of Victorian poetry, incurred the admiration of the great public of 'poetry readers' and 'lovers of verse' not so much because of its own merits, which were slender, but for two other reasons: in the first place because little intellectual effort was required to understand these lyrical outbursts; secondly, because the war, by providing a common background to thoughts and emotions, further accentuated the time-honoured worship of romantic geography by colouring it with the hues of patriotism. The tendency to intellectual laziness on the part of the public was still further encouraged by the growth of the anthology habit, by which means a choice of simple and easy pieces were flung together so that he who ran might read.

In the years that have followed the new books of important poetry may be numbered upon one hand. From the Georgian attitude there followed a reaction to what may be termed 'intellectuosity' on the part of the more noticeable poets. This intellectuosity may indeed have its vices, but it is at least provocative of thought, and it has in consequence proved refreshing to readers weary of the Georgian milk-and-soda. We do not intend, however, to analyse its ingredients here.

We would enquire firstly why there is so little good poetry, and secondly, why there is so little good criticism of poetry (or why such good criticism as there is should be so inaccessible)? The most obvious retort would seem to be that quality is always rare. So much must be granted. But it is also pertinent to draw attention to Mr. Philip Guedalla's observation that the best literary intellect of the younger generation tends toward subjects in which prose is the medium employed. For this inclination a multitude of reasons may be offered: 'poetry cannot deal with the ugliness of modern life; poetry cannot deal adequately with the most absorbing subjects of the day, which demand scientific analysis, etc., etc.' Such considerations are, of course, in some cases eminently reasonable, although it seems to us that the argument about 'beauty' and 'modern life' must be met with suspicion. Nor will we allow the contention that the decay of criticism derives from the decay of Poetry. Rather we maintain the reverse. If a man is not shown his faults, how shall we mend them? If his merits are not recognized, being human, how shall a Poet persevere? Is it not yours to guide us from the slough and set our feet aright? There are not wanting signs that such a need is already felt. The snobbery of some literary critics with regard to 'accepted' authors is, fortunately, widely recognized, but their frequent superficiality, their *incompetence*, their obviously unsympathetic (and by unsympathetic we would indicate not necessarily unfavourable attitudes but indifference to the aims and purposes the writers may have in view) and no less obviously *cursory* attention, their irrelevant remarks, their infelicitous attempts at humour, and their slick banalities, which they would nowadays so often pass off as 'literary criticism' – these should not be allowed to continue unrebuked.

For *pari passu* with the decay of criticism has dwindled the authority and value of Reviews. Seemingly in that would of affairs of which we dreamers as yet know little the great men who acquire newspapers as we used to collect cigarette cards, justly recognizing that Books are the Cinderella of commerce, hardly tolerate the intrusion of Literature among more lucrative interests, and prefer to reserve 'Drama' and 'Epic' to spice the trivial announcements in their headlines and posters.

No wonder if under such masters the Reviewer, grudgingly rewarded, adopts Protean habits, and multiplies with adroit variants his hasty judgements in half a dozen papers.

Critic, have we provoked you? Throw away the other five review copies of our aspirant verse, honest (we assure you) if poor, and read the sixth in the hope of enjoyment. Then assume your trenchant pen and set yourself

> *To tell us frankly of our foulest faults*
> *To laugh at our vain words and vainer thoughts.*
> (Good Dryden, condone our variants!)

But remember we look to you for guidance!

*The hungry sheep look up...*

# EDITORIAL

Since the character of any group or society is of necessity reflected in its literature; and since the idea would still seem to persist in the more remote parts of the world that Oxford is yet a home of culture, it is incumbent upon the Editors of so distinguished a journal as the OXFORD OUTLOOK to see to it that those who entertain this notion are not too rudely disillusioned.[1] As in the past so now, Cambridge, for instance, looks to us for fitting example; and indeed we, too, must look – and to our laurels; for they have talent in their Corpus and the Magdalene. We do not intend here to discuss the various vehicles of Oxford journalism (Heaven forbid that we should) but we wish to take this opportunity at the beginning of a new period of editorship, of giving some indication of the new policy of the Editors. In 1768 the founders of the *Oxford Magazine* (or *University Museum*) declared:

"Among other subjects of general entertainment, the authors propose to give... complete systems of every branch of useful learning, enriched with all the improvements of modern writers. They do not, however, propose to confine their labours entirely to the elucidation of the sciences; they propose to give a large account of the political and other transactions in different parts of the world, especially in our own country; every remarkable event, every uncommon debate, and every interesting turn of affairs will be recorded. A copious and authentic history of foreign and domestic occurrences will also be given, digested in a chronological series, containing all the material news of the month... the elegant amusements of literature, the flights of poetical fancy, and the brilliant sallies of inoffensive wit, shall find a place in our Magazine."

Our readers need not take alarm; our own ambitions do not stand so high. We are distinctly chary of the "flights of poetical fancy" – for the time being, at any rate. As for "uncommon debates," we have heard some strange things at the Union in our

---

[1] Parsons himself was editor of the *Oxford Outlook* in which this piece appeared.

time; and as for "domestic occurrences" we fear they would be mostly unprintable. Our plan is not quite so comprehensive. THE OUTLOOK will remain predominantly literary in character, but we shall seek to give expression in it to wider and more varied interests than have been treated in the past. Articles on the stage, therefore, or on modern art and music, on the Ballet, on literary movements and architectural developments or the records of interesting travel, will be welcome for the consideration of the eager and assiduous Editors. We therefore take leave of our astonished public for the time being, expecting a singular and felicitous concurrence of All The Talents in this University in order that we may grace its leisured with *literae vere humaniores*.

This fuss about *The Well of Loneliness*, a dull and dismal book, and Jix's announcement of his concern for "these little ones" have combined to cause anxiety in many honest minds.[2] Is this the beginning of a new censorship of literature by the Home Secretary and the Police? God save the mark! Shall we have to fight for our liberties afresh? We are not alarmed. The trouble about the book was to a certain extent accidental, to a certain extent provoked; and as to the Home Secretary's utterance, why should we take this more seriously than so many of his which we smile and forget?

---

[2] *The Well of Loneliness* was a novel written by Radclyffe Hall and first published in 1928. It gained notoriety for its treatment of the themes of lesbianism and homosexuality and, as a result of a censorious campaign by James Douglas editor of the *Sunday Express,* was banned in the United Kingdom until 1949. One of the key advocates for its censorship was the incumbent Home Secretary William Joynson-Hicks ('Jix') a man known for his socially conservative views even opposing a revised edition of *The Book of Common Prayer*. He referred to Radclyffe Hall's novel as being, 'gravely detrimental to the public interest.'

# "THESE GENTLEMEN CALL SUCH WRITING POETRY"

That there is nothing new under the sun is one of those aphorisms which call attention to certain particles of truth by containing in themselves more than a little falsehood. Consider art; while life is short, *it* is held to be "long", that is to say, enduring. Real art is enduring because it is intimately related to the life of the artist. The genuine artist does not deny the forces of tradition, indeed (particularly in youth) he will scarcely be able to escape the influence of such forces; nevertheless, if he is sincere he will always be beginning again at the beginning, and he will aim at tackling afresh the difficult problem of expression that "plus c'est la même chose, plus ça change." It would be unhistorical to maintain that there is no difference between the literary problems which faced early inhabitants of the Ionian Islands and those which face the inhabitants of modern London and New York. Certain instincts and desires – the unchanging elements of human nature – remain the same; but a whole host of mutative influences, a multiplicity of explorations and discoveries in the mental and material world have intervened, and probably no great writer or school of writers has passed away without introducing subtle changes into the language used. Unless we should be so foolish as to believe that the writing of verse should be a mere academic exercise to be executed in the void, after set patterns and examples, and with no relation to the intellectual temper of the author or of his age – somewhat in the manner of Latin and Greek verse composition at school – we shall hesitate to dismiss with an angry gesture of impatience of the arrival of any new literary forms, or any new modes of expression which may happen to differ from the forms and modes hitherto employed or which may happen to surprise the ear accustomed to other tones and phrases. The poet must derive much of his inspiration not only from what he thinks and reads, but also from what he sees and hears; and in our modern angular and syncopated world, with its many exciting and disturbing novelties and discoveries, it is the privilege of the dull and timid only to deprecate, in the spheres of literary, artistic, and musical creation, attempts at readjustment (even if unsuccessful) in the relations always existing between the creative impulse and circumambient phenomena. The crux of the difficulty lies in the fact that although the modern poet, as opposed to the conventional versifier, recognizes with peculiar intensity the truth of Mr. Aldous Huxley's remark, "that the badness of Wordsworth, like his goodness, is of all time," he has not yet discovered that unifying principle which gives his thought homogeneity. "The (modern) poet," says Sir Samuel Hoare[3], "if he is, as he must be, a man of intelligence, is compelled to form with the complexity of the modern world a host of relations, not merely physical or social, but also intellectual, which are easily resolvable into unity. He is torn in a number of directions: he has to exist on a great many planes of being. So has the ordinary person, but the difficulty for the modern poet is to take up an attitude in which these activities are synthesized. He has to reach a point from which the *whole* of the energies which seem to be dissipated in them can be transferred to poetic processes." What does in fact emerge from the contemplation of the best modern English and American poetry is firstly (this is naturally the feeling of any poet as opposed to metrical hackwriters), an acute sensitiveness to the depreciation of verbal currency due to the facile reproduction of the kind of worn and commonplace epithets which always find a ready welcome with such critics as "C.P."[4] of the *Manchester Guardian*; secondly, a kind of self-critical irony and intellectual self-consciousness in part suggestive of the secular poetry of the seventeenth century; thirdly an attitude of satirical detachment conveyed by reels of detailed photography. But let that pass; what we wish to urge is that whatever may be the prejudices and dogmas of critics dead-from-the-neck-up, Oxford must keep an open mind. Do not let us imitate the barbarians either within or without the gates. A journal of some standing in the University last term

---

[3] Sir Samuel Hoare (1880–1959) was a Conservative politician who served in various Cabinet posts in the Conservative and National governments in the 1920s and 1930s. He was briefly Foreign Secretary in 1935 and Home Secretary from 1937–1939.

[4] C.P refers here to C.P. Scott (1846–1932) who edited the *Manchester Guardian* from 1872 until 1929 and was its owner from 1907 until 1932. Between 1895 and 1906 he was also a Liberal MP.

suffered an extraordinary emission of personal and vulgar abuse to slobber across its pages. Mr. Denzil Batchelor's review of *Oxford Poetry* 1928 was a masterpiece of critical ineptitude and bad literary manners. We do not maintain that these poems were all of a high level, but we hoped that at least hostile critics would entertain us with some show of wit. Contempt is welcome provided it is expressed with literary grace. Disdain is almost to be courted when it is carried upon the wings of a fine prose style. The best effort towards humour (it appeared, we believe, either in the *Nation* or the *New Statesman*) was something about the capacity of the cellars in the British Museum; the author of this sally will no doubt be delighted to learn that, since the publication of *Oxford Poetry*, Messrs. Victor Gollancz have undertaken the publication of Mr. Louis MacNeice's poems. The volume is to be called *Blind Fireworks*.

Oxford may be the home of lost causes; the University, for instance, regularly returns a Conservative unopposed to the House of Commons. The rule of the Proctors is arbitrary and medieval and may easily in the hands of weak men with large ideas of their own importance, become unjust. But let us remember that it was also the home of the author of *Gaston de Latour* and of *Marius the Epicurean*.[5] If we cannot have the virtues as well as the vices while we are young, we shall never deserve to have those virtues in crabby old age.

---

[5] Both of these novels were written by Walter Pater and which adumbrated their author's belief in the need for an aesthetic life – one driven by the pursuit of sensation and insight.

# PURITY

Whatever system, or whatever absence of system in ethics, the English may have in practice observed, the moral code to which the greatest amount of lipservice has been paid and in accordance with which a minority have attempted to regulate their lives is the moral code elaborated in the New Testament by Jesus Christ. This is a startling fact, and not one which an uninstructed person would be inclined to deduce from a study of men's actions either at the present time or in the past. Nevertheless it is true that forms of Christianity have been the authoritative religions prevalent in the greater part of Europe for some twelve centuries and it is also true that on some occasions the incompatibilities between theory and practice have been noticed, and even commented upon, by men either wiser or more honest than the rest. I would not for a moment suggest that the chaplains and priests who have so often been ready to encourage perfectly unjustifiable manslaughter by telling soldiers that God alone – the militaristic deity of Mr. Rudyard Kipling on the Jehovah of the Old Testament – was certainly on their side and would see to it that they would win – I would not for a moment suggest that these chaplains and priests were all conscious of their own dishonesty, for though on Sundays they taught that the only way to achieve salvation was by obeying the Ten Commandments, it has always been clearly recognized among the clergy no less than among the laity, that there are in fact two religions, one for Sunday and one for the other days of the week; that though Christ may have preached the Sermon on the Mount, there were times when obedience to such doctrines might prove inconvenient to the State; and that if God could only perceive what was to them so patent, that *they* were in the right and that the enemy was in the wrong, and that hence it was their duty to kill as many of the evildoers as possible, He would be ready to condone a temporary departure from the exact observance of His Son's teaching. Therefore we need not expect to find the great majority of bishops and priests much troubled in their consciences about the morality of war, since in this matter they can easily let the State shoulder the burden of responsibility. But with regard to purity, it has been slightly otherwise. Indeed it is no exaggeration to say that it has been one of the chief functions, if not the *most* important function of the Christian religion to operate upon the sense of shame caused by lapses from purity – a sense of shame which, if it has not itself created, it has beyond all doubt served greatly to augment. Whether or no Christ intended it to be so, it is undeniable that among thousands of those who have boasted themselves His superior disciples, the very subject of sex itself has been regarded as a sinful matter. The ordinary physical desires of men and women have been twisted into fantastic and terrifying shapes; the instinct to copulate, as natural in a man as in a rabbit or a frog, has been exalted to the level of a deadly sin and symbolized in the Devil, while at the same time the various social and economic causes which do render a natural desire mercenary and pernicious have been disregarded as part of some grand incomprehensible scheme inaugurated by God to "try" the faith of men. The abnormal emphasis which Christianity has laid upon sex is well illustrated by the fact that out of fourteen meanings allotted to the word "pure" in Chambers's *Twentieth Century Dictionary,* the word "chaste" comes seventh in the list, and yet "chastity," or *sexual* purity, is certainly the first connotation which would arise in the minds of ninety-nine men out of a hundred confronted with the word.

The Sermon on the Mount paints a society which may rank with the finest of Utopias; and yet it is not difficult to see how dangerous in some respects are the normal effects of the altitude of its idealism. It is a curious and unfortunate thing that the professional "good" man (or Puritan) should have so often neglected those factors in Christianity which would have conduced to social well-being and felicity, persecuting instead and making life a tragedy for others because he does not believe that they are living up to the moral standards set by such a dictum as:

> "Whosoever looketh on a woman to lust after her hath committed adultery with her already in his heart."

This can mean only one thing, namely, any man who, looking at a woman, has at the same time thoughts of physical possession, is guilty of impurity. Whereupon we may justifiably enquire to what purpose "male and female created He them"? Reflections upon the fate of Sodom and Gomorrah prevent us from thinking that any other kind of sexual attraction would be preferable; and if desire at the sight of a woman is not to be accounted normal, desire provoked by the unaided imagination should be accounted of terrible consequence.

These observations are not prompted by erotomania, but by a conviction that the problem of sexual desire cannot be dismissed with a mere negative command: "Thou shalt not wish to sin." In the first place a greater degree of scepticism as to the validity of our judgments as to what constitutes "sin" or immorality than is entertained by the Puritan strongboys is necessary; and secondly where "sin" may be held undeniably to exist, medical science is a far more powerful instrument for the removal of impurity than the parrot-like repetitions of dogmatic injunctions.

With regard to the first point, as to what constitutes immorality, it is noticeable that while opinions may widely vary among different men, no impartial spectator can say that any set of men are of necessity *better* than others because of their holding certain opinions about morality. Christ drank wine with publicans and sinners. The Americans have gone one better than Christ and prohibit the consumption of wine. In the eyes of the American State, to drink alcohol is to sin. Here they agree with the Mohammedans; but whereas, among Mohammedans it is a sin to eat pork, Americans may eat as much pork as they like with impunity. For an American to have sexual intercourse with more than one woman during her life-time is regarded as sin (I am considering religious *theory*, of course), but among Mohammedans, who are not subject to the Christian sex complex, polygamy is altogether free from blame. Certain natives of India regard it as a sin to eat in public; certain tribes are matriarchies, where polyandry is the rule; and so on. Such examples prove, I think, that the sexual basis of purity in Europe is due to the prevalence of a certain kind of religion in that part of the world; but that to claim that monogamy, or marriage as at present established in England for example, constitutes the essence of "purity," and that all departures therefrom are "impure" is absurd. Not so many years ago, marriage to a deceased wife's sister was illegal in England – no doubt the nearness of relationship constituted "impurity"; but now such a marriage is legal and hence, we may suppose, perfectly "pure."

The fatal results of allowing any one man, or group of men, to set themselves up as censors of public morals and to persecute and imprison anyone who disagrees with his or her conceptions of purity are well illustrated by the astonishing career of Anthony Comstock[6]; for such men invariably end up, if they do not begin, by persecuting innocent persons and damaging the serious drama, art or literature of the people over whom they exercise their tyranny; while at the same time their efforts in the interest of purity serve only to give advertisement to, and increase the general interest in, pornography. "It is hardly possible," Mr. Broun quotes Sidney Smith, "that a society for the suppression of vice can ever be kept within the bounds of good sense and moderation... Beginning with the best intentions in the world, such societies must, in all probability, degenerate into a receptacle for every species of tittle-tattle, impertinence and malice. Men whose trade is rat-caching love to catch rats; the bug destroyer seizes upon the bug with delight; and the suppressor is gratified by finding his vice." So we find Comstock exulting that in forty-one years he had "convicted enough persons to fill a passenger train of sixty-one coaches, sixty coaches containing sixty passengers each and the sixty-first almost full. I have destroyed 160 tons of obscene literature" – not to mention the number of persons he drove to suicide.

Two American cartoons ably depict the prurient nature of Comstockery. In one, under the heading "That Fertile Imagination," Comstock is shown arresting an artist for depicting a woman almost totally submerged. "Don't you suppose I can't imagine what is under the water?" is Anthony's explanation; in the other, Comstock with enormous belly, is dragging a young woman before an infuriated judge. "Your Honour," says Comstock, holding up a forbidding finger, "this woman gave

---

[6] Anthony Comstock (1844–1915) was a United States Postal Inspector and politician who espoused staunchly Victorian moral values. He campaigned throughout his life to censor materials he declared obscene and indecent. Comstockery – a term first coined by the *New York Times* – became therefore a pejorative term for censorship and the restriction of free speech.

birth to a naked child." But there is another ingredient in the Puritan's interference with his neighbour and with the Press – psychological myopia. We may smile at Comstock draping the nude, and battling with Boccaccio, but we must remember that it was an Englishman who banned the production of *Mrs. Warren's Profession*[7] – not so many years ago – because, although an earnest sociological play, it dealt with the subject of prostitution. And in the present year, two esteemed gentlemen, the Home Secretary and Sir Chartres Biron, have startled all thoughtful men by suppressing *The Well of Loneliness*, a serious book and with patches of literary merit, because it deals with the question of the "masculine woman." By what arguments do these knights of purity justify their actions? They say that certain books are obscene because they would corrupt and deprave minds liable to depravity. They will therefore judge a book by tearing some lines from their context, and submitting them to somebody whose mind is already depraved, enquire "Do you find this passage obscene?"

The truth is that we are menaced with what Mr. Bertrand Russell, in one of his "Sceptical Essays" calls the "Recrudescence of Puritanism." The first thing that needs to be done is a revision of the obscenity laws – revision to be made not by people with minds prone to obscenity, nor yet by illiterate and ignorant Home Secretaries. The criterion of "offending one of these little ones" is ridiculous; and no less ridiculous is the practice of magistrates in refusing to listen to the advice of experts on the question of whether a book is or is not obscene. Do Sir William Joynson-Hicks and Sir Chartres Biron imagine that Mr. Bernard Shaw, Mr. H.G. Wells and Mr. John Galsworthy are really devoting themselves to the interests of pornography? "It is my own notion," says Mr. Heywood Broun[8], "that an ounce of

---

[7] *Mrs Warren's Profession* was a play written by George Bernard Shaw in 1893 and first performed in London in 1902. The nine year delay between completion and performance was due to it being banned by the Lord Chamberlain's Office (Britain's official theatre censor) due to its subject of prostitution.

[8] Heywood Broun (1888–1939) was an American journalist who founded the American Newspaper Guild. He wrote extensively on social ills and believed in the power of journalism to redress inequality.

sophistication is more valuable than many pounds of purity. The boy who shudders at the approach of smut is in greater danger than the one who can say, "I've heard that one, it isn't funny any more." Magistrates should be at liberty to order the suppression of "pornographic" literature when a committee of scientific and literary experts has pronounced it pornographic; but that it should be left to men incapable of forming a valid opinion on the matter to settle whether a book by Mr. James Joyce or Miss Radclyffe Hall should be read by the cultured public is not only an insult to the republic of letters, it is an attack on public liberties. It may be that the liberty of the Press will have to be again defended from the onslaught of men who forswear the principle of interference whenever and wherever it is really needed, but apply it – in the world of thought – in a manner that is both harmful and foolish. Purity! What sins have been committed in thy name! We may expect to see many more yet.

As for the second consideration suggested above, that the scientific treatment of acknowledged immortality is likely to achieve better results than repetition of formulae, that is a fact vaguely recognized by the Catholic church in its institution of confession of sins to a priest, but very definitely substantiated by the achievements of doctors and psycho-analysts. Indeed, the psycho-analyst can, by probing the mind of a professional Puritan, generally discover why it is he does more harm than good; it is often the case that disgusted with his own failures, he devotes all his energy to exhibiting what he considers the failure of others. The science of the mind is yet in its infancy, but it is making progress; and I believe it is to knowledge rather than to faith that all rational people must look for an effectual treatment of the vexed problems of morality.

# EDITORIAL BOUQUET

## MR. ROBERT BYRON[9] AND THE OXFORD PRESERVATION TRUST

We are much indebted to the editor of the *Architectural Review* for sending us the March number of that superfine magazine. Besides Mr. Martin Buckmaster's address on "Art in the Public Schools," a vigorous attack on the neglect of the study of painting, sculpture, music, and architecture in the Public Schools and Universities, recently delivered at the Headmasters' Conference, this number contains an article, "Oxford Revisited," illustrated with sarcastic photographs, by Mr. Robert Byron – which is such a witty and provocative criticism of the monstrosities of Oxford architecture that we would like to quote it almost in full. It should certainly be read by all the members of the Oxford Preservation Trust and by everyone interested in the doings of that well-intentioned body which has begun its work by encouraging the destruction of one of the finest medieval streets in England – St. Aldgate's. Mr. Byron is as equally indignant with the new statue of Mercury in Tom Quad, "perching in pseudo-classical incongruity upon a square gate-post... in the midst of the great green expanse, immutable, one had thoughts, in its Gothic austerity" as with the "labyrinths of semi-industrial slums" and "interminable vistas of fantastic but depressing villa residences" which the undergraduate must first traverse in order to take a country walk. "No longer," he writes, "do the spires and towers glimmer, as de Wint painted them, white and mirage-like from the fat elms and deep green water-meadows of the Thames Valley. Instead they pierce a smoke pall, fighting for predominate in the view with gasworks and chimney stacks. Villas dot the hills. Great sheds expand over the unresisting flats... also lamp-post standards, hoardings, petrol stations, the bric-a-brac of commercial England," Cooper's marmalade and Morris's motors

[9] Robert Byron (1905–1941) was a British dandy and travel writer best known for his account of his adventures in the Middle East *The Road to Oxiana*, first published in 1937. He was killed by a torpedo when on board a ship travelling to Egypt during the middle of the Second World War.

are national, nay imperial, benefits, but the foundation of similar industries may reasonably, without offence to patriotic virtue," so Mr. Byron argues, "be encouraged to arise in other and equally convenient localities."

All this is certainly familiar matter to the Trustees and to everyone else. But if one may put forward a personal opinion, there is also the possibility, is there not, of making a virtue of necessity. The Oxford of to-day is vastly different to the Oxford of seventy years ago, but to some undergraduates, industrial Oxford has its charms. Mr. W.H. Auden is said to have declared that the only place in Oxford where he could think was "by the gasworks." The walk by the river above Folly Bridge is one of the present editor's favourite walks; and the particular view of the gasometer which Mr. Byron has photographed with such aesthetic indignation (the photograph is reproduced in this number) is, he is obliged to confess, one of his favourite views in Oxford. Nevertheless, the undergraduate, because (generally) he does not visit these quarters, is inclined to forget that there are many slums and squalid streets in Oxford which are a disgrace both to the City and the University; and though we sympathize with Mr. Byron's opinion that when a new site is required, the authorities should demolish first of all, "a festering colony of Ruskinian villa residences or a block of offices and restaurants designed by an age gyrating in search of a taste like a cat its tail," we cannot agree with him. Villa residences may be hideous, but the squalor of slums is worse.

The gist of Mr. Byron's argument is that the Trust should not be called The Oxford *Preservation* Trust, because "they are concerned with the preservation of as ugly a blot of the English landscape can show. Their name and purpose should be changed to *Restoration*."

# OBSCENITY

> "On its pedestal of convenience the law still sits sedentary, costive, unable to bring forth common sense; and then when stirred into action, drunk with its old wine, aiming at a steady and consistent course, it wobbles and fails." – Laurence Housman[10]

Messrs. Wishart & Co. recently published an excellent book (the authors were Mr. Heywood Broun and Miss Margaret Leach) called *Anthony Comstock, Roundsman of the Lord*. It dealt with the curious career of a man who boasted that he had "convicted enough persons to fill a passenger train of sixty-one coaches, sixty coaches containing sixty passengers each and the sixty-first almost full. I have destroyed 160 tons of obscene literature" – to say nothing of the lives of those unfortunate and often mentally disordered people whom he drove to suicide. How wretched were the objects upon which Comstock expended his efforts and how great the amount of harm which resulted from his endeavours may be gathered from any intelligent account of his life. One is glad to notice that another enlightened book on the subject of "Obscenity" and the Censor has now been published – *To the Pure*, by Morris L. Ernst and William Seagle (Jonathan Cape) – of which a good short review has been written by Mr. Laurence Housman in Messrs. Cape's periodical *Now and Then* (No. 31). At a time when openly in Ireland, discretely in England, there are signs of an authoritative desire to undermine the liberties of the Press on specious charges of "indecency" and "obscenity," it is important that the whole problem of censorship should be openly and freely discussed with a view to the revision of the present laws on the subject. It should be more generally recognized that Queen Victoria no longer occupies the throne; Lord Justice Cockburn's fantastic definition of obscenity as that which tends "to deprave and corrupt those whose minds are open to depravity and corruption" no less than the rule which

---

[10] Laurence Housman (1865-1939) was the brother of the poet A.E. Housman and a noted illustrator and playwright in his own right. In addition, Housman was both a socialist and pacifist co-founding the Men's League for Women's Suffrage in 1907.

forbids a magistrate to consult the opinions of witnesses must certainly be relegated to the lumber-room – together with the last of the China dogs and the rest of "Aunt M's antimacassardom." Mr. Housman suggests that in order to extract its full flavour of absurdity from the Cockburn definition, one should substitute for "obscenity" some other word, such as, for example, "indigestibility." Thus we have: "The test of indigestibility is the tendency to cause indigestion in those whose constitutions make them liable to attacks of indigestion." Such a definition enforced by law would be the equivalent of a successful economic blockade. It is comforting to reflect, however, that an author may perhaps still escape persecution by dedicating his book to his mother; for in the heart of the most Puritan of Puritan strongboys there must lurk a soft spot, accessible to the more tender emotions.

# NOTES ON THE TEXT

"Introduction" to "Last Poem" comprise the volume *Poems* (1932).

"Paysages", "Débâcle" and "Fragment from Broken Ecstasy" first appeared in *Oxford Poetry*, 1927 edited by W.H. Auden and C. Day-Lewis (Oxford: Basil Blackwell)

"By Day the Green Wind Stirs", "Dancing", "English Winter-Piece" and "Plage Demimondaine" first appeared in *Oxford Poetry*, 1928 edited by Clere Parsons and B.B. (Oxford: Basil Blackwell)

"Colour-Photograph" (a later version entitled "Photogravure" appeared in *Poems*) and "Suburban Naturepiece" (a later version also appeared in *Poems*) first appeared in *Oxford Poetry*, 1929 edited by Louis MacNeice and Stephen Spender (Oxford: Basil Blackwell)

"The Morning Smells Chaste" first appeared in *The Oxford Outlook* June 1929, Vol X No. 49 edited by Clere Parsons.

"A Plea for Better Criticism" first appeared in *Oxford Poetry* 1928.

"Editorial" first appeared in *The Oxford Outlook* November 1928, Vol X No. 47 edited by Clere Parsons.

"These Gentlemen Call Such Writing Poetry" first appeared in *The Oxford Outlook* February 1929, Vol X No. 48 edited by Clere Parsons.

"Purity" first appeared in *Sir Galahad*, March 1929, No. 1

"Editorial Bouquet" first appeared in *The Oxford Outlook* June 1929 Vol X, No. 49

Parsons also published three book reviews in *The Oxford Outlook* and one book review in *The Criterion*, none of which are included here.